MW01608098

The Amazing (and Accurate) Adventures Of Chester Chipmunk

Based on a True Story

The Amazing (and Accurate) Adventures Of Chester Chipmunk

Based on a True Story

Lily Beth Linders

iUniverse®

THE AMAZING (AND ACCURATE)
ADVENTURES OF CHESTER CHIPMUNK
BASED ON A TRUE STORY

iUniverse books may be ordered through booksellers or by contacting:

iUniverse
1663 Liberty Drive
Bloomington, IN 47403
www.iuniverse.com
1-800-Authors (1-800-288-4677)

ISBN: 978-1-5320-3070-3 (sc)
ISBN: 978-1-5320-3069-7 (e)

Library of Congress Control Number: 2017913743

Print information available on the last page.

iUniverse rev. date: 10/19/2017

To the late Charlie Chickadee. May he rest
in peace. He was taken from us too soon.

Also to all my fur babies, past, present, and
future. They have made me laugh, they have made
me cry, and they have made my life so much
richer. I can't imagine my life without them in it.

Preface

The story you are about to read is absolutely 100 percent true—although I must confess that I can't actually know exactly what goes on in the minds of the critters featured here (for that I used my imagination). The events themselves did happen exactly as I have written them.

I hope that you enjoy reading this story as much as I enjoyed living (and writing) it!

Introduction

Welcome to my backyard—my peaceful, happy place. It's my place to relax, enjoy nature, and observe all the creatures who live there.

My yard is also the playground for my two pooches, Peanut and Pumpkin. They are crazy little Chihuahuas who love to run, chase anything that moves, and explore.

Unfortunately, it is also sometimes the hunting ground for my kitty, Freckle. In spite of my determined efforts to keep her indoors, Freckle is a very gifted escape artist. She waits patiently until that back door opens, and then *bam*—she's gone! This has led to my being on the receiving end of some very unpleasant and unwanted gifts.

This story, however, is a positive one. Its message is a hopeful one. It's about appreciating the freedom that we are so lucky to enjoy. It's about how important freedom is to all of us, whether we have two legs or four, fins or feathers. We all deserve to be free.

Chapter 1
Snatched!

It was a typical morning in the life of Chester Chipmunk, foraging for nuts to make sure his family would have a good supply to make it through another harsh Canadian winter. Chester often told his family how lucky they were to live in such a safe place, where the food was so plentiful thanks to the nice lady and her son, who always made sure that the bird feeders were full and the squirrels and chipmunks had a good supply of peanuts. Chester thought, *It's because of their kindness that our bellies are always full and we never need to worry about venturing into the wilderness to find enough to eat.*

He continued stuffing nuts into his already bursting cheeks. *I think that's enough for today. Time to head home to the wife and kids.* He sighed contentedly, thinking of his wife, Chelsea, and their five adorable kids, Chase, Chip, Chara, Chester Junior, and the baby Cherish. Chester was very proud of how well he provided for his little brood.

Then, in the blink of an eye, Chester's entire world was turned upside down. He was making his way back home when out of the bushes sprang a terrifying black-and-white monster. Chester was wide-eyed and cowered in fear. Although the monster made not a sound, its intentions were very clear. In an instant, the creature was upon Chester, and the chipmunk was firmly gripped between its sharp teeth. He fought valiantly through the pain, but to no avail. With his heart pounding wildly, his only thoughts were of his young family. *How will they survive without me there to care for them? Who will bring them food and make sure they are safe?*

He deeply regretted not telling them how much he loved them before he left earlier that morning, and he hoped that they knew.

The next thing he knew, he was fearfully facing a window that seemed to lead into the dwelling where the nice lady lived. As if on command, the window opened. *No!* thought Chester. *Please, please, please … Don't take me in there! What if I never make it out alive? What would happen to my family?* But struggling only made the grip on his neck tighten. The next thing he knew, the monster, with Chester in its powerful jaws, was inside.

Chester felt like a rag doll being tossed this way and that. He felt certain that his neck would snap at any moment. *Isn't there anyone who cares enough to help me?* he wondered as he felt himself slipping away. Through his closing eyes, he caught sight of a huge pair of sneakered feet. *What now?* he wondered. *Could things possibly get any worse?* His gaze travelled weakly up from the huge sneakers to find that they belonged to a gargantuan two-legged apparition who looked a lot like the nice lady who always made sure that the bird feeders were full and the squirrels and chipmunks had a good supply of peanuts. It was the nice lady's son!

Chester watched, amazed, as the apparition engaged in battle with the fearsome creature, screaming, "No, Freckle! Stop! Drop it, Freckle!" He picked something up from the floor and began to berate the monster. "No, Freckle! Stop!"

The monster named Freckle looked confused but loosened its grip. Chester fell limply to the floor. *Am I free? Is this nightmare over?* As weak as he was, he thought, *I have no time to waste. Somehow I have to find the strength to make my move. I have to find a way to get back to my family.*

He quickly darted into a dark room that was piled high with boxes of all shapes and sizes, including one low open box that was filled with what looked like sand. His nose twitched. *What is that smell?* he wondered, shuddering. The overpowering smell emanating from the box of sand reminded him of the black-and-white monster, and it made his eyes sting and his stomach turn.

The door to the room slammed shut, and Chester was trapped inside in total darkness. He was still trembling in fear thinking of what had almost happened to him. *I could so easily not have survived that attack. What will happen next? How can I possibly escape from this prison alive when I know the monster is waiting patiently on the other side of the door? I have to try to get through this. I have to try to get home.*

Chapter 2

Captivity

Chester's eyes flew open. A blinding light had woken him from a fitful, nightmare-filled sleep. Once again the two-legged apparition appeared. This time he started tossing the boxes all over the place, peering behind them, inside them, and under them. Chester was confused. *What is he doing now? He seems to be searching for something ... Could he be looking for me? Could he possibly be trying to help me again? But how can I know for sure?* But just when Chester thought maybe he should leave his hiding place and show himself, something appeared that made him freeze dead in his tracks. The black-and-white monster was right behind him!

Chester caught his breath and drew back as far as he could into his hidey-hole, but the cat quickly sniffed him out. It came closer and closer, crouching with ears flattened and tail twitching. Chester was certain that the cat was preparing to pounce, so he held his breath and stayed as still and as quiet as he could. *If I make myself as small as I possibly can, maybe it won't see me. But I'm sure the creature must be able to hear my heart pounding—it feels like it's going to burst right out of my chest.*

Once again the oddly helpful two-legged apparition came to Chester's rescue and managed to shoo the menacing monster out of the room. But before he left, he placed a small bowl of water and a dish of peanuts on the floor. *Is that for me?* Chester wondered. *Why does this strange person keep trying to save me? I just don't understand.*

Chester waited a few moments to make sure the coast was clear, and then he crept cautiously over to the bowls and dug in. *I didn't realize how hungry I was. I've been too busy just trying to stay alive to even think about food. But these nuts sure are tasty.* He gobbled up as many nuts as his tummy could handle and slurped down the fresh water until his thirst was quenched. Then, once again in total darkness, he slipped back into his hiding place. Chester felt a little stronger now that he was no longer hungry. He felt himself getting a little bit calmer, and he was definitely a lot sleepier.

Days passed, but how many—Chester had no idea. *It's so dark in here that I can't tell whether it's day or night. I'm losing track of time,* he worried.

Although he did manage to sustain himself thanks to the food that his kind rescuer had left, he could feel himself getting weaker. He could feel his spirit and his will to live fading away. He thought sadly, *What is the point of living without my family, without my friends, and without my freedom?* He found himself drifting in and out of sleep. Sometimes he dreamed he was out in the sunshine, collecting nuts or playing with his children; other times he had vivid nightmares of vicious monsters stealing him away and taking him to a place he could never escape from alive. Those nightmares left him feeling desperate, and his heart beat wildly as he panted for breath.

After what felt like an eternity, Chester was once again startled awake. He peered cautiously out into the room. The door had opened again, and Chester didn't understand what was going on when it stayed open. *But where is the monster? Has my rescuer given up on me? Does he think I'm dead? What should I do now?* Chester thought carefully about what his next move should be. *I must not hurry. I must bide my time. I must make sure that it's safe before I try to make my escape.* In his little hiding place, he waited and waited until finally he couldn't wait any longer. He dared to venture forth from the room that had been his prison. *What will I find on the other side of the door?* he wondered. He had no idea, but he vowed that he would find out. Chester tried to prepare himself. *I will face whatever comes my way with as much courage and strength as I can muster. I just have to keep thinking about my family and my real life on the outside.*

Quiet as a mouse, he crept slowly into another room and saw that his new friend and savior was sleeping soundly, snoring softly. Unfortunately, the monster was curled snugly by his side, contentedly purring away. Chester caught sight of something on the floor beside the bed that made him stop cold. He felt his knees buckle and his stomach lurch. He quickly saw that it was the lifeless body of a harmless bird. *Oh no! That's my friend Charlie Chickadee!* Charlie Chickadee would always make sure to drop some tasty treats from his perch on the bird feeder when he saw that Chester was foraging in the yard.

Chester was horrified and knew for sure who was responsible for this. *How can this be? Charlie did nothing to deserve this! He was a good bird. He would never even hurt a fly. And what if I'm next?*

That cat is surely out to get me. He shuddered, said a silent farewell to his friend, and raced out of that room as fast as his little legs would allow.

He bounded up a series of steps and found himself in what seemed to be a totally different world. It was bright and cheery, not dark, dreary, and frightening like the downstairs. He cautiously sniffed around, trying to get his bearings in this new place, and he found a fireplace with a hot fire warming the room. Next to the fireplace was a fragrant pile of wood. *This is the perfect spot for me to hide!* The smell of the logs and the crackling fire filled his nostrils and even reminded him a little bit of his home. *Finally! A safe place for me to rest. If I can rest, maybe I can find the strength to keep going. I have to keep going. I have to find my way back, somehow ...* Exhausted, he settled in and felt himself nodding off. As he slept this time, only beautiful visions of his wife, his children, his friends, and his home filled his dreams.

Chapter 3

Now What?

Just as he finally allowed himself to rest, to sleep peacefully in a place where he believed he could feel somewhat secure, Chester was jolted awake. *What is that sound?* It was a sound that sent chills through his entire body and made him quake with fear. It was the sound of angry barking, and the sound was getting closer by the second. *Good heavens. Now what?* he thought. *How much more can one little chipmunk take? I'm so tired and so weak. I'm not sure I can keep going. Why do these horrible things keep happening to me?*

Chester's thoughts flew back to the time of his kidnapping. He had thought that the creature who took him then was the most terrifying and evil creature he had ever seen. But the two who were approaching him now, making those evil noises, were even more frightening and even larger—much larger. The hackles on their backs were raised, and their teeth were bared. Chester felt certain that this was it. *It's all over for me now. There is no possible way that I can escape from this.* He bravely stood, puffed out his chest, and prepared himself to meet his fate with dignity.

The nice lady, who always made sure that the bird feeders were full and the squirrels and chipmunks had a good supply of peanuts, rushed in to save him. Chester now knew she was called Mom because the two-legged apparition who had helped him so many times had called her that. She quickly called to the two angry animals, identifying them as Peanut and Pumpkin. Somehow she managed to encourage them to leave the house through the back door. *The nice lady named Mom is very crafty!* Chester thought. She enticed them with treats, and something about that word made them forget all about the little chipmunk cowering in the woodpile. Drooling and with tongues lolling, they obediently followed Mom outside. *They may be scary, but they're certainly not very bright,* Chester thought.

Chester breathed another sigh of relief. *Whew! That was another close one! It's so strange how these two-legged beings keep coming to my rescue. I'm not sure why they seem so intent on saving me, but I'm most definitely grateful that they are! I'm so thankful that they always seem to be right there whenever and wherever I need them.* He knew that he would have been doomed if it was not for their help. *I still don't really understand, though. How do they know? Are they watching me?*

Once again, Chester scrambled to find a place to hide. *I am so tired of hiding. I'm tired of running. I'm just so tired.* Oh, how he missed the freedom of running through the grass, the feel of the dew on his feet in the morning, the taste of the newly fallen rain. *Will I ever have the chance to experience any of these things again? Will I ever see my family again? Are they worrying about me? Are they hungry? Do they miss me as much as I miss them? And, worst of all, do they think I'm gone for good?* All these thoughts made Chester feel very sad and very helpless. Chester was not used to feeling helpless; he was used to being in charge.

Chester found himself again forced into hiding. But for some reason there was a constant supply of nuts and water. *No one has ever brought me food and water before. No one has ever tried to care for me. I'm the one who looks after everyone. I'm the one who is strong. I'm the provider.* It was a strange feeling to have someone taking care of him. It wasn't quite as horrible as before in that basement, but it certainly wasn't home.

Chapter 4

Courage!

One day Chester was drawn out of hiding by an irresistible smell that made his mouth water and his tummy growl. He built up the nerve to leave the dark place where he had been hiding. He climbed and climbed, and then he climbed even higher. While standing on his little hind legs, he stretched as high as he could and sniffed at the jar he found on the counter. He sniffed and sniffed and thought, *No way! I must have died and gone to heaven!* What he was sniffing appeared to be a jar full of … *No, it can't be! Peanut butter! It simply cannot get any better than this!* Except, of course, it could get better than that. *It would be much better if I were sharing it with my family.* But he dug in anyway, the peanut butter sticky in his mouth. *I have to take my food when I can get it because I know I have to try to keep up my strength so that I can get out of here.*

As he stuffed himself with peanut butter, his lips smacking, Chester thought, *One thing I know for sure now is that all good things usually come to an end.* It was a matter of time before this good thing came to an end too.

Mom spied Chester on the counter as he was clinging to the rim of the peanut butter jar. "Oh!" exclaimed Mom.

"Squeak!" exclaimed Chester. Oddly enough, Mom burst out laughing. She laughed so hard that she was almost crying. But she quickly collected herself and seemed to be trying to make him understand that she simply wanted to help him. She spoke softly to him as she approached with her hand outstretched, and she made little clucking noises. "Shh, little chipmunk. I won't hurt you. I just want to help you get out of here."

But Chester didn't understand the language that she was speaking, and he was far too frightened to listen to her pleas. *I have to hide again! I have to find a safe place to hide!* He flew across the counter, leaped down, and once again disappeared.

From his hiding spot, Chester watched as Mom went to the cupboard and took out a huge bag of peanuts. He watched as she carefully started placing the nuts in a trail from the countertop by the window to the peanut butter jar and down to the floor near where Chester hid. He watched as she opened the window over the sink, and he watched as she removed the screen from the window. Then he watched as she quietly left the room.

Chester was afraid to venture once again into the unknown, but he was much more afraid of never getting out of there. *That's all I want. I just want to be free again. Free to enjoy my family. Free to enjoy spending time with my friends. Free to enjoy my life as a free chipmunk. Is that too much to ask?*

Chester made his decision. He decided it was time to swallow his fear and to once again attempt to secure his freedom. He steeled himself, took a deep breath, and followed that trail of nuts.

He climbed way up to where he had found the jar of peanut butter, and then he found the opening where the screen had been removed by Mom to leave him with a doorway to the outside world. He carefully climbed up onto the windowsill and warily stepped out into the world—his world, the world from which he had been so brutally wrenched. It was the world he had been dreaming of returning to for those dark, fear-filled days.

Chester breathed in deeply, revelling in the fresh air of the yard. He listened to the familiar sounds of the birds and the wind and all the creatures he knew so well. *I have never in my entire life smelled anything more wonderful than this. It smells better than seeds, better than nuts, and even better than peanut butter!* He paused and once again filled his lungs. He pinched himself. *I must be dreaming! But If I am dreaming, I really hope that I never wake up!*

But for some reason Chester felt torn. It had been terrifying, yes. It had been confusing as well. And yet there had been those nuts and the water that had magically appeared whenever he needed them the most. *Maybe I should stay. It was kind of nice to have someone look after me for a change. I feel that Mom and her son really cared about me and were trying to help me.* Chester thought hard about what he should do. *The problem is I would never know when a terrifying four-legged creature could appear who wants nothing more than to enjoy me as a tasty snack. And of course I would never see my family again.*

Chester made his decision. He took one last look back at the place where he had been so frightened and yet had somehow been so cared for. He noticed Mom, who was watching him wavering on the ledge, and she smiled at him. She seemed to be saying, "You can do it, little chipmunk. You can do it!" Chester smiled back at Mom, and then he jumped as fast and as far as he could. He jumped for joy, he jumped for love, and he jumped for freedom.

Chapter 5

Freedom!

Once Chester landed and had all four feet firmly planted on the ground again, he ran as if the black-and-white monster was once again trying to capture him. *I can't believe I made it out of there alive! I can't believe it!* He ran and ran straight into the arms of his beloved family. Chester had never felt such joy.

Chester's wife, Chelsea, could not believe that Chester had returned to them. She had assumed the worst. After all, he had been missing for five long days. "Where have you been?" she demanded. "How could you have left us for so long?" She cried tears of joy that streaked her furry cheeks. The kids raced in happy circles around their dad, jumping on his back and clinging to his legs.

All the other chipmunk families in the neighbourhood heard the commotion coming from the Chipster home and came crowding around to investigate. "Is that Chester?" "No way! Chester was a goner!" "It is Chester!" "I can't believe it!" "Holy cow! Chester's back!" On and on they chattered.

Finally quiet settled over the little group. Chester slowly and softly recounted the story of his amazing (and accurate) adventures. He told them of his capture and of all the terrifying things he had encountered over the course of the five days that he had been missing. He told them of his escape. He said, "But I must also tell you of the kindness of the nice lady named Mom, who always made sure that the bird feeders are full and the squirrels and chipmunks have a good supply of peanuts. I must also tell you of the kindness of the gargantuan two-legged apparition who is Mom's son."

Chester continued with his story. "Every time I was ready to give up, ready to let myself fade away, there would always magically appear a supply of nuts and water no matter where I was hiding." He told of how the nice lady had opened a door to the outside world and left a trail of nuts to show him the way. He told them how she had smiled encouragingly at him as he hesitated on the windowsill. He then told them of his giant leap of faith, the leap of faith that he had taken because he felt that he must return to his family.

All the chipmunk families sat wide-eyed and spellbound as Chester told the story of his amazing (and accurate) adventures. They simply could not believe that his story was true. How could it possibly be true? And yet this was Chester, and Chester had always been truthful. He had always been brave. And so they began to believe.

Chelsea shouted out to the crowd, "We need to prepare a huge feast with all the bells and whistles! We need to celebrate my husband's miraculous return to us!"

The Chipster family's close friend Chucky piped up. "And we totally need to have a spectacular chipmunk parade!" Chucky was always looking for a reason to have a spectacular chipmunk parade. He loved them more than anything.

As they scurried about making preparations, gathering food for the feast, planning the spectacular chipmunk parade, chattering away merrily, and laughing happily, Chester allowed himself to relax for the first time in five long days. Those were the longest five days of his entire life. He reflected on the decision he had been forced to make: whether to stay put and enjoy the comforts provided by Mom and her son, or to do everything he could to make his escape. Whether to enjoy burrowing into the fragrant woodpile and enjoy the heat from the fire burning beside it or to risk his life trying to get back outside. Chester now knew that he had made the right decision. "There may have been lots to eat and drink, and there may have been those who would help me and care for me, and it may have been warm and cozy—but it would never have felt like my home. This is my home. This is where I belong."

And so he watched, listened, and allowed himself to just be—to be content, unafraid, and happy. He allowed himself to take in the sights and sounds of his beloved family and his many dear friends.

He revelled in the taste of the one thing he had missed above all else: his freedom.

Chester's Biography

Actual photo of Chester's escape!

Chester was born and raised in the backyard of a small but comfortable home located on a road called Reynolds in a city called London, Ontario. He married his childhood sweetheart, Chelsea, and they had too many children and grandchildren to count.

The story of his amazing (and accurate) adventures would be recounted for years to come to generation after generation of chipmunk families.

Chester will always be remembered for his bravery and courage, for his strength, and for his loyalty to all who knew and loved him.

Lily Beth's Biography

Lily Beth was born and raised in a small but comfortable home located in London, Ontario. She had three children, all sons, and so far she has no grandchildren. She has had too many careers to name and has lived in too many places to count.

Lily Beth would like to be remembered for her love of all animals, for her love of freedom, and for her love of laughter.

Printed in the United States
By Bookmasters